ENDANGERED ANIMALS

SOUTH AMERICA

Grace Jones

Image Credits

All images are courtesy of Shutterstock.com, unless otherwise specified. With thanks to Getty Images, Thinkstock Photo and iStockphoto.
Front Cover – Mikadun. ostill. Eric Gevaer. 1 – Fotos593. 4&5 – SAHACHATZ, Neale Cousland. 6&7 – Rich Carey, Patryk Kosmider, Dennis van de Water. 8&9 – Johnny Lye, Dr Morley Read. 10&11 – Anan Kaewkhammul, Ammit Jack, Andrea Izzott, Neil Burton, Anan Kaewkhammul, Berendje Photography, Fotos593, ostill, Ondrej Prosicky, nastenkin. 12&13 – By Fernando Flores (Own work) [CC BY-SA 3.0 (http://creativecommons.org/licenses/by-sa/3.0)], via Wikimedia Commons, Nagel Photography. 14&15 – Jamen Percy, Rich Carey, nwdph. 16&17 – Fons Vermeulen, Chris Hill, Eric Gevaert. 18&19 – Neil Burton, lovemelovemypic, scnhnc052008. 20&21 – JT Platt, Ryan M. Bolton, Christian Vinces. 22&23 – Ondrej Prosicky, mythja, Jiri Vondrous. 24&25 – Janelle Lugge, JT Platt, worldswildlifewonders. 26&27 – Marius Dobilas, Rawpixel.com, Sam DCruz, Shvaygert Ekaterina, wavebreakmedia, Oscity.

BookLife
PUBLISHING

©2018
BookLife Publishing
King's Lynn
Norfolk PE30 4LS

A catalogue record for this book is available from the British Library.

ISBN: 978-1-78637-247-5

Written by:
Grace Jones

Edited by:
Kirsty Holmes

Designed by:
Drue Rintoul

CONTENTS

Words that look like this are explained in the glossary on page 30.

ENDANGERED ANIMALS

Experts estimate that there are anywhere between two million and nine million **species** living on planet Earth today, but thousands of these are in danger of dying out every single year.

WHAT DOES IT MEAN IF A SPECIES IS ENDANGERED?

Any species of plant or animal that is at risk of dying out completely is said to be endangered. When all individuals of a single species die, that species has become extinct. Extinction is a real possibility for all species that are already threatened or endangered. Experts estimate that between 150 and 200 different species become extinct every day.

Dinosaurs are an example of an extinct species. They walked the Earth over 225 million years ago and became extinct around 65 million years ago.

4

The International Union for Conservation of Nature and Natural Resources (IUCN) is the main **organisation** that records which species are in danger of extinction. The species are put into different categories, from the most to the least threatened by extinction.

IUCN'S CATEGORIES OF THREATENED ANIMALS

Category	Explanation
Extinct	Species that have no surviving members
Extinct in the Wild	Species with surviving members only in **captivity**
Critically Endangered	Species that have an extremely high risk of extinction in the wild
Endangered	Species that have a high risk of extinction in the wild
Vulnerable	Species that are likely to become endangered or critically endangered in the near future
Near Threatened	Species that are likely to become vulnerable or endangered in the near future
Least Concern	Species that fit into none of the above categories

The Javan rhinoceros has been categorised by the IUCN as 'critically endangered', with around 46-66 individuals remaining in the wild.

The IUCN's work is extremely important. Once a species has been recognised as 'at risk', organisations and **governments** will often take steps to protect the species and its **habitats** in order to save it from extinction. The practice of protecting or saving a species and its habitats is called **conservation**.

WHY DO ANIMALS BECOME ENDANGERED?

Over the last 100 years, the human **population** of the world has grown by over 4.5 billion people. As the population has grown, the damage humans do to the **environment** and wildlife has increased too. Many experts believe that human activity is the biggest threat to animals around the world today.

Habitat Destruction

One of the biggest threats species face is the loss of their habitats. Large areas of land are often used to build **settlements** to provide more housing, food and **natural resources** for the growing world population. This can often destroy natural habitats, which nearby wildlife need in order to survive.

THE WORLD WIDE FUND FOR NATURE (WWF) ESTIMATES THAT BETWEEN 200 AND 2,000 SPECIES OF ANIMAL BECOME EXTINCT EVERY SINGLE YEAR.

To use land for housing or farming, all the trees must be cut down and cleared from the area. This is called **deforestation**.

POLLUTION

Pollution is the introduction of harmful waste to the air, water or land. Pollution threatens wildlife all over the world. For example, people drop litter, which can cut, choke or even poison animals.

Hunters and Poachers

Many species are endangered because of hunting or **poaching**. Humans throughout history have hunted certain species of animal for their meat, furs, skins or tusks.

The dodo was a species of bird that was hunted to extinction. The last time a dodo was seen alive was in 1662.

Male African elephants are hunted by poachers for their huge tusks, which are made from a natural material called ivory and are sold for lots of money.

NATURAL CAUSES

While the most serious threats to animals are caused by humans, there are natural threats to animals too. For example, it is thought that the extinction of the dinosaurs was caused by a natural event, when a **meteorite** hit the Earth. Other species may become extinct because they are not as well **adapted** to survive in their environments as others. Experts believe that the number of species that become extinct due to human activity is around 1,000 times more than those becoming extinct through natural causes.

SOUTH AMERICA

South America is one of the seven continents of the world. Continents are large areas of land that, along with five oceans, cover the Earth. The other six continents are: Africa, Antarctica, Asia, Australia, Europe and North America. South America is the fourth-biggest continent in the world. It is located to the south of North America and to the west of Africa. There are two oceans that surround South America. The Atlantic Ocean lies on the east coast of South America and the Pacific Ocean on the west.

CONTINENTS OF THE WORLD

DO YOU KNOW WHICH CONTINENT YOU LIVE IN?

ARCTIC OCEAN

ASIA

EUROPE

NORTH AMERICA

ATLANTIC OCEAN

PACIFIC OCEAN

AFRICA

PACIFIC OCEAN

SOUTH AMERICA

INDIAN OCEAN

AUSTRALIA

ANTARCTIC OCEAN

ANTARCTICA

FACTS ABOUT SOUTH AMERICA

FACTFILE

Population: Over 425 million people.

Land Area: Over 17.8 million square kilometres (km).

Countries: 12

Highest Peak: Aconcagua in Argentina rises to 6,961 metres (m) above sea level and is located in the Andes mountain range.

Longest River: The River Amazon is the second longest river in the world and is over 6,400 km long.

Biggest Country by Area: Brazil is over 8.5 million square km and covers over half of the continent.

Main Language Spoken: Spanish

River Amazon

Amazon Rainforest

WILDLIFE AND HABITATS

There are many different types of habitat found across the South American continent, from tropical rainforests to deserts, mountains and **marine** habitats. The Amazon rainforest covers around one-third of the entire continent and is home to one of the largest ranges of wildlife on Earth. There are lots of different species here; 427 species of mammal, 1,300 bird species, 378 reptile species, 400 amphibian species, 3,000 fish species and more than 40,000 species of plant!

ENDANGERED SOUTH AMERICAN ANIMALS

In 2013, the IUCN listed over 2,600 species as threatened or endangered in South America, and many of these live in the Amazon rainforest. Deforestation, **urban** development and farming are responsible for large-scale habitat destruction, which threatens thousands of species across South America.

10 ANIMALS IN DANGER IN SOUTH AMERICA

1

Orinoco Crocodile

Conservation Status:
Critically Endangered

Number:
Between 250–1,500

2

Jaguar

Conservation Status:
Near Threatened

Number:
Around 15,000

3

Golden Lion Tamarin

Conservation Status:
Endangered

Number:
Around 1,000 adults in the wild

4

Galápagos Penguin

Conservation Status:
Endangered

Number:
Around 1,200 adults in the wild

(5)

Giant Otter

Conservation Status:
Endangered

Number:
Unknown

(6)

Margay

Conservation Status:
Near Threatened

Number:
Around 64

(7)

Manatee

Conservation Status:
Vulnerable

Number:
Between 8,000–30,000
adults in the wild

(8)

Waved Albatross

Conservation Status:
Critically Endangered

Number:
Fewer than 36,000
adults in the wild

(9)

Maned Wolf

Conservation Status:
Near Threatened

Number:
Around 17,000 adults in
the wild

(10)

Broad-Snouted Caiman

Conservation Status:
Least Concern

Number:
Unknown

ORINOCO CROCODILE

FACTFILE

Number Living in the Wild: Between 250–1,500

IUCN Status: Critically Endangered

Scientific Name: *Crocodylus intermedius*

Weight: Males usually weigh around 380 kilograms (kg) and females around 200 kg

Size: Males can reach up to 6 m long and females up to 4 m long

Life Span: Up to 80 years

Habitat: savannas and freshwater rivers

Diet: Carnivore

Orinoco Crocodile

Where Do They Live?

Orinoco crocodiles are now only found in and around the Orinoco river in Venezuela and Colombia.

Key

- Oceans and Seas
- Land
- Orinoco Crocodile Habitats

SOUTH AMERICA

Pacific Ocean

Atlantic Ocean

WHY ARE THEY IN DANGER?

Orinoco crocodiles were hunted to near extinction during the 19th and 20th centuries. They were hunted for their valuable skin, which people use to make things, like bags and shoes. Now, Orinoco crocodiles are also **illegally** hunted for their meat and their teeth, which in some countries are believed to have **medicinal properties**.

Today there are only between 250 and 1,500 Orinoco crocodiles left in the wild.

How Are They Being Protected?

The Convention of International Trade in Endangered Species (CITES) has banned the **trade** of crocodile skin and teeth. Even though the species is protected in many areas, the laws that protect it are often not strictly enforced, and illegal poaching is still common. In the 1990s, in Venezuela, a programme to reintroduce captive Orinoco crocodiles back into the wild began. Today, there are at least six **captive breeding programmes** and many baby crocodiles have been released back into the wild over recent years.

JAGUAR

FACTFILE

Number Living in the Wild: Around 15,000

IUCN Status: Near Threatened

Scientific Name: *Panthera Onca*

Weight: Between 45–95 kg

Size: Between 1–1.9 m long

Life Span: Around 12 years

Habitat: Forests, rainforests, grasslands and swamps

Diet: Carnivore

Jaguar

Where Do They Live?

Jaguars prefer to live near water; in forests, rainforests, grasslands and swamps. They used to live all over South America and in many parts of North America too. Now there are none left in southern parts of South America, and only a few in North America.

Key

Oceans and Seas

Land

Jaguar Habitats

SOUTH AMERICA

Pacific Ocean

Atlantic Ocean

Why Are They in Danger?

One of the biggest threats that jaguars face is habitat destruction. Large-scale deforestation in South America has pushed jaguars into smaller and smaller areas in which to live. Often deforestation has occurred in order to make space for urban development or farming, which has meant the species has come into more **conflict** with humans. Some jaguars kill farmers' **livestock** and, although it is illegal to kill them, they are often shot and killed for this reason.

JAGUARS ARE ALSO HUNTED FOR THEIR PAWS, FUR AND TEETH.

HOW ARE THEY BEING PROTECTED?

According to CITES, the hunting of jaguars is illegal across most of their range, including Argentina, Brazil and Colombia. A conservation program has also begun to protect a strip of land from the very north to the very south of the species' range.

However, jaguars live across many thousands of kilometres, and protecting large areas of land across many countries can be difficult. A joint conservation effort is needed to make sure the species is saved from future extinction.

GOLDEN LION TAMARIN

FACTFILE

Number Living in the Wild: Around 1,000 adults

IUCN Status: Endangered

Scientific Name: *Leontopithecus rosalia*

Weight: 6-11 kg

Size: Between 15-25 centimetres (cm) long

Life Span: Up to 8 years in the wild

Habitat: Rainforests

Diet: Omnivore

Golden Lion Tamarin

Where Do They Live?

Golden lion tamarins live in very small areas in rainforests on the Atlantic coast of Brazil.

Pacific Ocean

SOUTH AMERICA

Atlantic Ocean

Key

Oceans and Seas

Land

Lion Tamarin Habitats

WHY ARE THEY IN DANGER?

Since the 16th century, deforestation has occurred in Brazil in order to use the land to grow sugar cane and coffee plantations and, more recently, for livestock and urban development. This has meant that golden lion tamarins have been pushed into a few small areas of rainforest habitat in Brazil. Around 90% of their original habitat has been destroyed by deforestation.

Some golden lion tamarins are also illegally captured to be sold on as pets in the animal trade.

How Are They Being Protected?

The Golden Lion Tamarin Conservation Programme was set up in 1983. Over the last 24 years, conservation efforts have focused on **breeding** the species in captivity, protecting the species' remaining habitats and reintroducing members bred in captivity back into the wild. Because of these conservation efforts, in the past 30 years the number of wild golden lion tamarins has grown from around 200 to 1,000 members and there are over 480 members currently in captivity.

WAVED ALBATROSS

FACTFILE

Number Living in the Wild: Fewer than 36,000 adults

IUCN Status: Critically Endangered

Scientific Name: *Phoebastria irrorata*

Weight: Between 3-5 kg

Wingspan: Between 2-2.5 m

Life Span: Up to 45 years

Habitat: Marine habitats to look for food and **scrublands** to breed and raise young

Diet: Carnivore

Waved Albatross

Where Do They Live?

Waved albatrosses live in two big **colonies** in marine habitats and scrublands. They live in and around two islands called Española Island and Isla de la Plata. These are part of the Galápagos Islands and are found off the coast of Ecuador.

Key

Oceans and Seas

Land

Waved Albatross Habitats

SOUTH AMERICA

Pacific Ocean

Atlantic Ocean

Why Are They in Danger?

Commercial fisheries fish in the waters of the Pacific Ocean where waved albatrosses look for and catch their food, which is usually fish, squid and **crustaceans**. This has left the species with less food to feed themselves and their young, which has caused the **survival rate** to decrease over recent years. Waved albatrosses can also easily become caught by **baited** hooks in a type of net that commercial fisheries use, and often die as a result.

An example of the type of hook used in the nets that can kill waved albatrosses.

HOW ARE THEY BEING PROTECTED?

In 2007, the Agreement for the Conservation of Albatrosses and Petrels organised workshops in Peru and Ecuador to develop a conservation action plan for waved albatrosses. Although fishing is banned on Española Island, the plan focuses on protecting more marine habitats within the Galápagos National Park and Marine Reserve. By increasing the number of protected areas, they hope to stop the damaging effects of overfishing on waved albatrosses.

GIANT OTTER

FACTFILE

Number Living in the Wild: Unknown

IUCN Status: Endangered

Scientific Name: *Pteronura brasiliensis*

Weight: Around 35 kg

Size: Up to 1.8 m long

Life Span: Around 12 years in the wild

Habitat: Large, slow-moving rivers, streams, lakes and swamps

Diet: Carnivore

Giant Otters

Where Do They Live?

Giant otters live in large, slow-moving rivers, streams, lakes and swamps in the Orinoco, Amazonas and Parana **basins**.

Key

Oceans and Seas

Land

Giant Otter Habitats

SOUTH AMERICA

Pacific Ocean

Atlantic Ocean

WHY ARE THEY IN DANGER?

The biggest threat giant otters face comes from gold mining. Gold miners often destroy river banks in order to find gold. Because otters make their homes, called dens, in river banks, gold mining has destroyed many giant otter habitats. Gold miners use a metal called mercury to join pieces of gold together. The mercury has contaminated the water habitats the otters live in and killed the fish that the otters rely on as their main food source.

This man is gold mining along the Madre de Dios riverbank in Peru.

How Are They Being Protected?

A ten-year conservation action plan is currently being developed. Conservation actions that have been suggested so far include creating new protected areas in giant otter habitats and better protecting ones that already exist. Conservationists also hope to train new otter tourist guides in order to better protect giant otters. The money that they make from wildlife tourism will help to fund conservation efforts in the future.

MARGAY

FACTFILE

Number Living in the Wild: Around 64

IUCN Status: Near Threatened

Scientific Name: *Leopardus wiedii*

Weight: 4-10 kg

Size: Between 85-132 cm

Life Span: Around 10 years in the wild

Habitat: Forest habitats

Diet: Carnivore

Margay

Where Do They Live?

Margays live in forest habitats in Brazil, Argentina, Paraguay, Uruguay and many other countries in South America. They also live in parts of the North American continent including Mexico, Costa Rica and Belize.

Key

- Oceans and Seas
- Land
- Margay Habitats

SOUTH AMERICA

Pacific Ocean

Atlantic Ocean

Why Are They in Danger?

One of the biggest threats to margays is illegal hunting. Margays have been hunted in the past few decades for their unusual fur, and captured alive to be sold as pets in the animal trade. It is estimated that around 14,000 margays were killed for their fur every year between 1976 and 1984. Margay numbers are also being affected by deforestation and habitat loss in recent years.

Margay fur would often be used to make fur coats like these.

HOW ARE THEY BEING PROTECTED?

CITES have banned the international trade and hunting of margays. However, illegal hunting is still a problem in some areas and countries. Margays are also still illegally captured to be sold on in the pet trade. Little is known about margays, so conservation programmes such as Project Wild Cats of Brazil are aiming to find out more in order to better protect the species and its habitats in the future.

CONSERVATION EFFORTS IN SOUTH AMERICA

Many steps have already been taken to protect wildlife and conserve habitats throughout South America, but much more can still be done to save endangered animals from future extinction.

Reforestation

Before 1990, deforestation was mostly uncontrolled across many countries in South America. Because of this, the biggest threat species face comes from habitat destruction. Throughout South America there are conservation projects that help to replant young trees and plants into areas that have been cleared, which recreates a habitat for wildlife to live in again. This process is called 'reforestation'. In Argentina, around 6,000 school children and their parents have planted an estimated 200,000 trees since 2008. With more conservation projects like these, we could bring back habitats and save thousands of species from extinction in the future.

LAWS AND GOVERNMENTS

Much progress has been made to save South America's wildlife by legally protecting the habitats of animals. However, there are 12 countries in South America, and they all have different laws and governments. Often, even if it is illegal to hunt animals, the law is sometimes not followed and the people who commit the crimes might not be caught or punished. For animals such as the margay and the jaguar, who are often illegally hunted, their future survival depends on countries working together to make sure that illegal hunting is stopped entirely.

Wildlife Tourism

Many wildlife organisations, charities and governments around the world are using the money that is made from wildlife tourism to protect endangered animals throughout South America. For example, new giant otter tourist guides are being trained to help better protect the species (see page 21 for more details). The money that is made from wildlife tourism will go towards funding conservation efforts in the future, which will hopefully help to save many species from extinction.

HOW CAN I MAKE A DIFFERENCE?

1 CAMPAIGN WITH AN ORGANISATION

Wildlife organisations such as WWF and Greenpeace have helped to save many endangered species, and even convince countries to change their laws through campaigning.

2 DONATE TO A CHARITY YOU BELIEVE IN

You can usually donate as little or as much as you want. Most charities show you how your donations are helping to make a difference.

3 LEARN MORE ABOUT ENDANGERED SPECIES IN YOUR AREA

One of the most important ways to protect endangered species is by understanding the threats that they face. Visit a local wildlife refuge, national park or reserve, or join a local wildlife organisation.

4 ADOPT AN ANIMAL

Your donation will normally go to feeding and looking after the animal that you have adopted. You'll usually get an adoption certificate and regular updates on how your animal is doing.

5 HELP TO RAISE AWARENESS BY TALKING TO OTHERS

It is important that we all talk about issues that may threaten wildlife throughout the world. By talking about these issues, it can help to make people aware of how they may be affecting wildlife and tell them how they can help.

6 VOLUNTEER AT A LOCAL WILDLIFE CHARITY OR SHELTER

It is not only endangered animals who need our help; we should help to take care of all the animals in the world.

FIND OUT MORE

To find out more about endangered species in South America and what you can do to get involved with conservation efforts, visit:

International Union for Conservation of Nature (IUCN)
www.iucnredlist.org

International Society for Endangered Cats (ISEC)
www.wildcatconservation.org/wild-cats/south-america

Save the Golden Lion Tamarin
www.savetheliontamarin.org

World Wide Fund for Nature (WWF)
www.worldwildlife.org

To discover more about other endangered animals around the world, take a look at more books in this series:

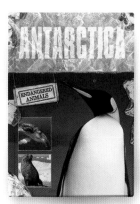
Antarctica, Endangered Animals
Grace Jones (BookLife, 2018)

Asia, Endangered Animals
Grace Jones (BookLife, 2018)

Australia, Endangered Animals
Grace Jones (BookLife, 2018)

Europe, Endangered Animals
Grace Jones (BookLife, 2018)

North America, Endangered Animals
Grace Jones (BookLife, 2018)

Africa, Endangered Animals
Grace Jones (BookLife, 2018)

QUICK QUIZ

1. HOW MANY ORINOCO CROCODILES ARE LIVING IN THE WILD?

2. WHAT IS THE SCIENTIFIC NAME OF THE JAGUAR?

3. WHAT DO WAVED ALBATROSSES FEED ON?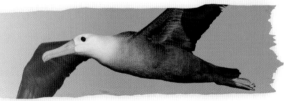

4. HOW MUCH DO GIANT OTTERS WEIGH?

5. HOW LONG DO MARGAYS USUALLY LIVE FOR?

6. WHAT IS THE IUCN CONSERVATION STATUS OF THE GOLDEN LION TAMARIN?

For answers see the bottom of page 32.

GLOSSARY

adapted	changed over time to suit different conditions
baited	to have attached bait to a hook in order to catch fish
basins	natural places containing water
breeding	the process of producing young
captive breeding programmes	programmes focused on producing young from animals that are cared for by humans
captivity	animals that are cared for by humans and not living in the wild
carnivore	animals that eat other animals rather than plants
colonies	groups of the same species of animal that live together
commercial fisheries	fishing companies who make money from large-scale fishing
conflict	active disagreement between people
conservation	the practice of protecting or conserving a species and its habitats
conservationists	people who act for the protection of wildlife and the environment
contaminated	made unclean by adding a poisonous or polluting substance to it
crustaceans	types of animal that live in water and have hard outer shells around their bodies
deforestation	the action of cutting down trees on large areas of land

environment	the natural world
governments	groups of people with the authority to run countries and decide their laws
habitats	the natural environments in which animals or plants live
illegally	performed outside of the limits of the law
livestock	animals that are kept for farming purposes
marine	relating to the sea
medicinal properties	thought to heal or cure illnesses
meteorite	a piece of rock that successfully enters a planet's atmosphere without being destroyed
mining	the act or process of extracting something, such as gold
natural resources	useful materials that are created by nature
omnivore	an animal that eats plants and other animals
organisation	a group of people that work together to achieve the same goals
poaching	the act of the illegal capturing or killing of wild animals
population	the number of people living in a place
savannas	flat areas of land covered with grass and with few trees
scrublands	lands with shrubs or small trees on them
settlements	places people live permanently, like villages or towns
species	a group of very similar animals or plants that are capable of producing young together
survival rate	the percentage of members of a species that die
trade	to buy and sell goods
urban	relating to a city or town
wildlife tourism	the actions and industry behind attracting people to visit new places to see wildlife

INDEX

1. Between 250–1,500 **2.** Panthera Onca **3.** Fish, squid and crustaceans
4. Around 35 kg **5.** Around 10 years in the wild **6.** Endangered